This Notebook
belongs to:

Contacts

Name	**Name**
Address	Address
City State Zip	City State Zip
Phone	Phone
Email	Email
Name	**Name**
Address	Address
City State Zip	City State Zip
Phone	Phone
Email	Email
Name	**Name**
Address	Address
City State Zip	City State Zip
Phone	Phone
Email	Email
Name	**Name**
Address	Address
City State Zip	City State Zip
Phone	Phone
Email	Email
Name	**Name**
Address	Address
City State Zip	City State Zip
Phone	Phone
Email	Email

Contacts

Name

Address

City   State   Zip

Phone

Email

Name

Address

City   State   Zip

Phone

Email

Name

Address

City   State   Zip

Phone

Email

Name

Address

City   State   Zip

Phone

Email

Name

Address

City   State   Zip

Phone

Email

Name

Address

City   State   Zip

Phone

Email

Name

Address

City   State   Zip

Phone

Email

Name

Address

City   State   Zip

Phone

Email

Name

Address

City   State   Zip

Phone

Email

Name

Address

City   State   Zip

Phone

Email

Contacts

Name

Address

City   State   Zip

Phone

Email

Name

Address

City   State   Zip

Phone

Email

Name

Address

City   State   Zip

Phone

Email

Name

Address

City   State   Zip

Phone

Email

Name

Address

City   State   Zip

Phone

Email

Name

Address

City   State   Zip

Phone

Email

Name

Address

City   State   Zip

Phone

Email

Name

Address

City   State   Zip

Phone

Email

Name

Address

City   State   Zip

Phone

Email

Name

Address

City   State   Zip

Phone

Email

Contacts

Name

Address

City   State   Zip

Phone

Email

Name

Address

City   State   Zip

Phone

Email

Name

Address

City   State   Zip

Phone

Email

Name

Address

City   State   Zip

Phone

Email

Name

Address

City   State   Zip

Phone

Email

Name

Address

City   State   Zip

Phone

Email

Name

Address

City   State   Zip

Phone

Email

Name

Address

City   State   Zip

Phone

Email

Name

Address

City   State   Zip

Phone

Email

Name

Address

City   State   Zip

Phone

Email

Contacts

Name

Address

City   State   Zip

Phone

Email

Name

Address

City   State   Zip

Phone

Email

Name

Address

City   State   Zip

Phone

Email

Name

Address

City   State   Zip

Phone

Email

Name

Address

City   State   Zip

Phone

Email

Name

Address

City   State   Zip

Phone

Email

Name

Address

City   State   Zip

Phone

Email

Name

Address

City   State   Zip

Phone

Email

Name

Address

City   State   Zip

Phone

Email

Name

Address

City   State   Zip

Phone

Email

Contacts

Name

Address

City   State   Zip

Phone

Email

Name

Address

City   State   Zip

Phone

Email

Name

Address

City   State   Zip

Phone

Email

Name

Address

City   State   Zip

Phone

Email

Name

Address

City   State   Zip

Phone

Email

Name

Address

City   State   Zip

Phone

Email

Name

Address

City   State   Zip

Phone

Email

Name

Address

City   State   Zip

Phone

Email

Name

Address

City   State   Zip

Phone

Email

Name

Address

City   State   Zip

Phone

Email

Contacts

Name

Address

City   State   Zip

Phone

Email

Name

Address

City   State   Zip

Phone

Email

Name

Address

City   State   Zip

Phone

Email

Name

Address

City   State   Zip

Phone

Email

Name

Address

City   State   Zip

Phone

Email

Name

Address

City   State   Zip

Phone

Email

Name

Address

City   State   Zip

Phone

Email

Name

Address

City   State   Zip

Phone

Email

Name

Address

City   State   Zip

Phone

Email

Name

Address

City   State   Zip

Phone

Email

Contacts

Name

Address

City   State   Zip

Phone

Email

Name

Address

City   State   Zip

Phone

Email

Name

Address

City   State   Zip

Phone

Email

Name

Address

City   State   Zip

Phone

Email

Name

Address

City   State   Zip

Phone

Email

Name

Address

City   State   Zip

Phone

Email

Name

Address

City   State   Zip

Phone

Email

Name

Address

City   State   Zip

Phone

Email

Name

Address

City   State   Zip

Phone

Email

Name

Address

City   State   Zip

Phone

Email

Contacts

Name

Address

City   State   Zip

Phone

Email

Name

Address

City   State   Zip

Phone

Email

Name

Address

City   State   Zip

Phone

Email

Name

Address

City   State   Zip

Phone

Email

Name

Address

City   State   Zip

Phone

Email

Name

Address

City   State   Zip

Phone

Email

Name

Address

City   State   Zip

Phone

Email

Name

Address

City   State   Zip

Phone

Email

Name

Address

City   State   Zip

Phone

Email

Name

Address

City   State   Zip

Phone

Email

Contacts

Name

Address

City   State   Zip

Phone

Email

Name

Address

City   State   Zip

Phone

Email

Name

Address

City   State   Zip

Phone

Email

Name

Address

City   State   Zip

Phone

Email

Name

Address

City   State   Zip

Phone

Email

Name

Address

City   State   Zip

Phone

Email

Name

Address

City   State   Zip

Phone

Email

Name

Address

City   State   Zip

Phone

Email

Name

Address

City   State   Zip

Phone

Email

Name

Address

City   State   Zip

Phone

Email

Contacts

Name

Address

City   State   Zip

Phone

Email

Name

Address

City   State   Zip

Phone

Email

Name

Address

City   State   Zip

Phone

Email

Name

Address

City   State   Zip

Phone

Email

Name

Address

City   State   Zip

Phone

Email

Name

Address

City   State   Zip

Phone

Email

Name

Address

City   State   Zip

Phone

Email

Name

Address

City   State   Zip

Phone

Email

Name

Address

City   State   Zip

Phone

Email

Name

Address

City   State   Zip

Phone

Email

Contacts

Name

Address

City   State   Zip

Phone

Email

Name

Address

City   State   Zip

Phone

Email

Name

Address

City   State   Zip

Phone

Email

Name

Address

City   State   Zip

Phone

Email

Name

Address

City   State   Zip

Phone

Email

Name

Address

City   State   Zip

Phone

Email

Name

Address

City   State   Zip

Phone

Email

Name

Address

City   State   Zip

Phone

Email

Name

Address

City   State   Zip

Phone

Email

Name

Address

City   State   Zip

Phone

Email

Contacts

Name

Address

City   State   Zip

Phone

Email

Name

Address

City   State   Zip

Phone

Email

Name

Address

City   State   Zip

Phone

Email

Name

Address

City   State   Zip

Phone

Email

Name

Address

City   State   Zip

Phone

Email

Name

Address

City   State   Zip

Phone

Email

Name

Address

City   State   Zip

Phone

Email

Name

Address

City   State   Zip

Phone

Email

Name

Address

City   State   Zip

Phone

Email

Name

Address

City   State   Zip

Phone

Email

Contacts

Name	Name
Address	Address
City State Zip	City State Zip
Phone	Phone
Email	Email

Name	Name
Address	Address
City State Zip	City State Zip
Phone	Phone
Email	Email

Name	Name
Address	Address
City State Zip	City State Zip
Phone	Phone
Email	Email

Name	Name
Address	Address
City State Zip	City State Zip
Phone	Phone
Email	Email

Name	Name
Address	Address
City State Zip	City State Zip
Phone	Phone
Email	Email

Contacts

Name

Address

City   State   Zip

Phone

Email

Name

Address

City   State   Zip

Phone

Email

Name

Address

City   State   Zip

Phone

Email

Name

Address

City   State   Zip

Phone

Email

Name

Address

City   State   Zip

Phone

Email

Name

Address

City   State   Zip

Phone

Email

Name

Address

City   State   Zip

Phone

Email

Name

Address

City   State   Zip

Phone

Email

Name

Address

City   State   Zip

Phone

Email

Name

Address

City   State   Zip

Phone

Email

Contacts

Name

Address

City   State   Zip

Phone

Email

Name

Address

City   State   Zip

Phone

Email

Name

Address

City   State   Zip

Phone

Email

Name

Address

City   State   Zip

Phone

Email

Name

Address

City   State   Zip

Phone

Email

Name

Address

City   State   Zip

Phone

Email

Name

Address

City   State   Zip

Phone

Email

Name

Address

City   State   Zip

Phone

Email

Name

Address

City   State   Zip

Phone

Email

Name

Address

City   State   Zip

Phone

Email

Contacts

Name

Address

City   State   Zip

Phone

Email

Name

Address

City   State   Zip

Phone

Email

Name

Address

City   State   Zip

Phone

Email

Name

Address

City   State   Zip

Phone

Email

Name

Address

City   State   Zip

Phone

Email

Name

Address

City   State   Zip

Phone

Email

Name

Address

City   State   Zip

Phone

Email

Name

Address

City   State   Zip

Phone

Email

Name

Address

City   State   Zip

Phone

Email

Name

Address

City   State   Zip

Phone

Email

Contacts

Name

Address

City   State   Zip

Phone

Email

Name

Address

City   State   Zip

Phone

Email

Name

Address

City   State   Zip

Phone

Email

Name

Address

City   State   Zip

Phone

Email

Name

Address

City   State   Zip

Phone

Email

Name

Address

City   State   Zip

Phone

Email

Name

Address

City   State   Zip

Phone

Email

Name

Address

City   State   Zip

Phone

Email

Name

Address

City   State   Zip

Phone

Email

Name

Address

City   State   Zip

Phone

Email

Contacts

Name

Address

City   State   Zip

Phone

Email

Name

Address

City   State   Zip

Phone

Email

Name

Address

City   State   Zip

Phone

Email

Name

Address

City   State   Zip

Phone

Email

Name

Address

City   State   Zip

Phone

Email

Name

Address

City   State   Zip

Phone

Email

Name

Address

City   State   Zip

Phone

Email

Name

Address

City   State   Zip

Phone

Email

Name

Address

City   State   Zip

Phone

Email

Name

Address

City   State   Zip

Phone

Email

Contacts

Name

Address

City   State   Zip

Phone

Email

Name

Address

City   State   Zip

Phone

Email

Name

Address

City   State   Zip

Phone

Email

Name

Address

City   State   Zip

Phone

Email

Name

Address

City   State   Zip

Phone

Email

Name

Address

City   State   Zip

Phone

Email

Name

Address

City   State   Zip

Phone

Email

Name

Address

City   State   Zip

Phone

Email

Name

Address

City   State   Zip

Phone

Email

Name

Address

City   State   Zip

Phone

Email

Contacts

Name

Address

City   State   Zip

Phone

Email

Name

Address

City   State   Zip

Phone

Email

Name

Address

City   State   Zip

Phone

Email

Name

Address

City   State   Zip

Phone

Email

Name

Address

City   State   Zip

Phone

Email

Name

Address

City   State   Zip

Phone

Email

Name

Address

City   State   Zip

Phone

Email

Name

Address

City   State   Zip

Phone

Email

Name

Address

City   State   Zip

Phone

Email

Name

Address

City   State   Zip

Phone

Email

Contacts

Name

Address

City   State   Zip

Phone

Email

Name

Address

City   State   Zip

Phone

Email

Name

Address

City   State   Zip

Phone

Email

Name

Address

City   State   Zip

Phone

Email

Name

Address

City   State   Zip

Phone

Email

Name

Address

City   State   Zip

Phone

Email

Name

Address

City   State   Zip

Phone

Email

Name

Address

City   State   Zip

Phone

Email

Name

Address

City   State   Zip

Phone

Email

Name

Address

City   State   Zip

Phone

Email

Contacts

Name

Address

City   State   Zip

Phone

Email

Name

Address

City   State   Zip

Phone

Email

Name

Address

City   State   Zip

Phone

Email

Name

Address

City   State   Zip

Phone

Email

Name

Address

City   State   Zip

Phone

Email

Name

Address

City   State   Zip

Phone

Email

Name

Address

City   State   Zip

Phone

Email

Name

Address

City   State   Zip

Phone

Email

Name

Address

City   State   Zip

Phone

Email

Name

Address

City   State   Zip

Phone

Email

Contacts

Name

Address

City　　　　　State　　　Zip

Phone

Email

Name

Address

City　　　　　State　　　Zip

Phone

Email

Name

Address

City　　　　　State　　　Zip

Phone

Email

Name

Address

City　　　　　State　　　Zip

Phone

Email

Name

Address

City　　　　　State　　　Zip

Phone

Email

Name

Address

City　　　　　State　　　Zip

Phone

Email

Name

Address

City　　　　　State　　　Zip

Phone

Email

Name

Address

City　　　　　State　　　Zip

Phone

Email

Name

Address

City　　　　　State　　　Zip

Phone

Email

Name

Address

City　　　　　State　　　Zip

Phone

Email

Contacts

Name

Address

City   State   Zip

Phone

Email

Name

Address

City   State   Zip

Phone

Email

Name

Address

City   State   Zip

Phone

Email

Name

Address

City   State   Zip

Phone

Email

Name

Address

City   State   Zip

Phone

Email

Name

Address

City   State   Zip

Phone

Email

Name

Address

City   State   Zip

Phone

Email

Name

Address

City   State   Zip

Phone

Email

Name

Address

City   State   Zip

Phone

Email

Name

Address

City   State   Zip

Phone

Email

Contacts

Name

Address

City   State   Zip

Phone

Email

Name

Address

City   State   Zip

Phone

Email

Name

Address

City   State   Zip

Phone

Email

Name

Address

City   State   Zip

Phone

Email

Name

Address

City   State   Zip

Phone

Email

Name

Address

City   State   Zip

Phone

Email

Name

Address

City   State   Zip

Phone

Email

Name

Address

City   State   Zip

Phone

Email

Name

Address

City   State   Zip

Phone

Email

Name

Address

City   State   Zip

Phone

Email

Contacts

Name

Address

City _____ State _____ Zip _____

Phone

Email

Name

Address

City _____ State _____ Zip _____

Phone

Email

Name

Address

City _____ State _____ Zip _____

Phone

Email

Name

Address

City _____ State _____ Zip _____

Phone

Email

Name

Address

City _____ State _____ Zip _____

Phone

Email

Name

Address

City _____ State _____ Zip _____

Phone

Email

Name

Address

City _____ State _____ Zip _____

Phone

Email

Name

Address

City _____ State _____ Zip _____

Phone

Email

Name

Address

City _____ State _____ Zip _____

Phone

Email

Name

Address

City _____ State _____ Zip _____

Phone

Email

Contacts

Name

Address

City   State   Zip

Phone

Email

Name

Address

City   State   Zip

Phone

Email

Name

Address

City   State   Zip

Phone

Email

Name

Address

City   State   Zip

Phone

Email

Name

Address

City   State   Zip

Phone

Email

Name

Address

City   State   Zip

Phone

Email

Name

Address

City   State   Zip

Phone

Email

Name

Address

City   State   Zip

Phone

Email

Name

Address

City   State   Zip

Phone

Email

Name

Address

City   State   Zip

Phone

Email

Contacts

Name

Address

City   State   Zip

Phone

Email

Name

Address

City   State   Zip

Phone

Email

Name

Address

City   State   Zip

Phone

Email

Name

Address

City   State   Zip

Phone

Email

Name

Address

City   State   Zip

Phone

Email

Name

Address

City   State   Zip

Phone

Email

Name

Address

City   State   Zip

Phone

Email

Name

Address

City   State   Zip

Phone

Email

Name

Address

City   State   Zip

Phone

Email

Name

Address

City   State   Zip

Phone

Email

Contacts

Name

Address

City   State   Zip

Phone

Email

Name

Address

City   State   Zip

Phone

Email

Name

Address

City   State   Zip

Phone

Email

Name

Address

City   State   Zip

Phone

Email

Name

Address

City   State   Zip

Phone

Email

Name

Address

City   State   Zip

Phone

Email

Name

Address

City   State   Zip

Phone

Email

Name

Address

City   State   Zip

Phone

Email

Name

Address

City   State   Zip

Phone

Email

Name

Address

City   State   Zip

Phone

Email

Contacts

Name

Address

City   State   Zip

Phone

Email

Name

Address

City   State   Zip

Phone

Email

Name

Address

City   State   Zip

Phone

Email

Name

Address

City   State   Zip

Phone

Email

Name

Address

City   State   Zip

Phone

Email

Name

Address

City   State   Zip

Phone

Email

Name

Address

City   State   Zip

Phone

Email

Name

Address

City   State   Zip

Phone

Email

Name

Address

City   State   Zip

Phone

Email

Name

Address

City   State   Zip

Phone

Email

Contacts

Name

Address

City   State   Zip

Phone

Email

Name

Address

City   State   Zip

Phone

Email

Name

Address

City   State   Zip

Phone

Email

Name

Address

City   State   Zip

Phone

Email

Name

Address

City   State   Zip

Phone

Email

Name

Address

City   State   Zip

Phone

Email

Name

Address

City   State   Zip

Phone

Email

Name

Address

City   State   Zip

Phone

Email

Name

Address

City   State   Zip

Phone

Email

Name

Address

City   State   Zip

Phone

Email

Contacts

Name

Address

City　　　　　State　　　Zip

Phone

Email

Name

Address

City　　　　　State　　　Zip

Phone

Email

Name

Address

City　　　　　State　　　Zip

Phone

Email

Name

Address

City　　　　　State　　　Zip

Phone

Email

Name

Address

City　　　　　State　　　Zip

Phone

Email

Name

Address

City　　　　　State　　　Zip

Phone

Email

Name

Address

City　　　　　State　　　Zip

Phone

Email

Name

Address

City　　　　　State　　　Zip

Phone

Email

Name

Address

City　　　　　State　　　Zip

Phone

Email

Name

Address

City　　　　　State　　　Zip

Phone

Email

Contacts

Name

Address

City　　　　　State　　　Zip

Phone

Email

Name

Address

City　　　　　State　　　Zip

Phone

Email

Name

Address

City　　　　　State　　　Zip

Phone

Email

Name

Address

City　　　　　State　　　Zip

Phone

Email

Name

Address

City　　　　　State　　　Zip

Phone

Email

Name

Address

City　　　　　State　　　Zip

Phone

Email

Name

Address

City　　　　　State　　　Zip

Phone

Email

Name

Address

City　　　　　State　　　Zip

Phone

Email

Name

Address

City　　　　　State　　　Zip

Phone

Email

Name

Address

City　　　　　State　　　Zip

Phone

Email

Contacts

Name

Address

City   State   Zip

Phone

Email

Name

Address

City   State   Zip

Phone

Email

Name

Address

City   State   Zip

Phone

Email

Name

Address

City   State   Zip

Phone

Email

Name

Address

City   State   Zip

Phone

Email

Name

Address

City   State   Zip

Phone

Email

Name

Address

City   State   Zip

Phone

Email

Name

Address

City   State   Zip

Phone

Email

Name

Address

City   State   Zip

Phone

Email

Name

Address

City   State   Zip

Phone

Email

Contacts

Name

Address

City   State   Zip

Phone

Email

Name

Address

City   State   Zip

Phone

Email

Name

Address

City   State   Zip

Phone

Email

Name

Address

City   State   Zip

Phone

Email

Name

Address

City   State   Zip

Phone

Email

Name

Address

City   State   Zip

Phone

Email

Name

Address

City   State   Zip

Phone

Email

Name

Address

City   State   Zip

Phone

Email

Name

Address

City   State   Zip

Phone

Email

Name

Address

City   State   Zip

Phone

Email

Contacts

Name

Address

City   State   Zip

Phone

Email

Name

Address

City   State   Zip

Phone

Email

Name

Address

City   State   Zip

Phone

Email

Name

Address

City   State   Zip

Phone

Email

Name

Address

City   State   Zip

Phone

Email

Name

Address

City   State   Zip

Phone

Email

Name

Address

City   State   Zip

Phone

Email

Name

Address

City   State   Zip

Phone

Email

Name

Address

City   State   Zip

Phone

Email

Name

Address

City   State   Zip

Phone

Email

Contacts

Name

Address

City   State   Zip

Phone

Email

Name

Address

City   State   Zip

Phone

Email

Name

Address

City   State   Zip

Phone

Email

Name

Address

City   State   Zip

Phone

Email

Name

Address

City   State   Zip

Phone

Email

Name

Address

City   State   Zip

Phone

Email

Name

Address

City   State   Zip

Phone

Email

Name

Address

City   State   Zip

Phone

Email

Name

Address

City   State   Zip

Phone

Email

Name

Address

City   State   Zip

Phone

Email

Contacts

Name

Address

City   State   Zip

Phone

Email

Name

Address

City   State   Zip

Phone

Email

Name

Address

City   State   Zip

Phone

Email

Name

Address

City   State   Zip

Phone

Email

Name

Address

City   State   Zip

Phone

Email

Name

Address

City   State   Zip

Phone

Email

Name

Address

City   State   Zip

Phone

Email

Name

Address

City   State   Zip

Phone

Email

Name

Address

City   State   Zip

Phone

Email

Name

Address

City   State   Zip

Phone

Email

Contacts

Name

Address

City   State   Zip

Phone

Email

Name

Address

City   State   Zip

Phone

Email

Name

Address

City   State   Zip

Phone

Email

Name

Address

City   State   Zip

Phone

Email

Name

Address

City   State   Zip

Phone

Email

Name

Address

City   State   Zip

Phone

Email

Name

Address

City   State   Zip

Phone

Email

Name

Address

City   State   Zip

Phone

Email

Name

Address

City   State   Zip

Phone

Email

Name

Address

City   State   Zip

Phone

Email

Contacts

Name

Address

City   State   Zip

Phone

Email

Name

Address

City   State   Zip

Phone

Email

Name

Address

City   State   Zip

Phone

Email

Name

Address

City   State   Zip

Phone

Email

Name

Address

City   State   Zip

Phone

Email

Name

Address

City   State   Zip

Phone

Email

Name

Address

City   State   Zip

Phone

Email

Name

Address

City   State   Zip

Phone

Email

Name

Address

City   State   Zip

Phone

Email

Name

Address

City   State   Zip

Phone

Email

Contacts

Name			Name		
Address			Address		
City	State	Zip	City	State	Zip
Phone			Phone		
Email			Email		

Name			Name		
Address			Address		
City	State	Zip	City	State	Zip
Phone			Phone		
Email			Email		

Name			Name		
Address			Address		
City	State	Zip	City	State	Zip
Phone			Phone		
Email			Email		

Name			Name		
Address			Address		
City	State	Zip	City	State	Zip
Phone			Phone		
Email			Email		

Name			Name		
Address			Address		
City	State	Zip	City	State	Zip
Phone			Phone		
Email			Email		

Contacts

Name

Address

City   State   Zip

Phone

Email

Name

Address

City   State   Zip

Phone

Email

Name

Address

City   State   Zip

Phone

Email

Name

Address

City   State   Zip

Phone

Email

Name

Address

City   State   Zip

Phone

Email

Name

Address

City   State   Zip

Phone

Email

Name

Address

City   State   Zip

Phone

Email

Name

Address

City   State   Zip

Phone

Email

Name

Address

City   State   Zip

Phone

Email

Name

Address

City   State   Zip

Phone

Email

Contacts

Name

Address

City   State   Zip

Phone

Email

Name

Address

City   State   Zip

Phone

Email

Name

Address

City   State   Zip

Phone

Email

Name

Address

City   State   Zip

Phone

Email

Name

Address

City   State   Zip

Phone

Email

Name

Address

City   State   Zip

Phone

Email

Name

Address

City   State   Zip

Phone

Email

Name

Address

City   State   Zip

Phone

Email

Name

Address

City   State   Zip

Phone

Email

Name

Address

City   State   Zip

Phone

Email

Contacts

Name

Address

City   State   Zip

Phone

Email

Name

Address

City   State   Zip

Phone

Email

Name

Address

City   State   Zip

Phone

Email

Name

Address

City   State   Zip

Phone

Email

Name

Address

City   State   Zip

Phone

Email

Name

Address

City   State   Zip

Phone

Email

Name

Address

City   State   Zip

Phone

Email

Name

Address

City   State   Zip

Phone

Email

Name

Address

City   State   Zip

Phone

Email

Name

Address

City   State   Zip

Phone

Email

Contacts

Name

Address

City   State   Zip

Phone

Email

Name

Address

City   State   Zip

Phone

Email

Name

Address

City   State   Zip

Phone

Email

Name

Address

City   State   Zip

Phone

Email

Name

Address

City   State   Zip

Phone

Email

Name

Address

City   State   Zip

Phone

Email

Name

Address

City   State   Zip

Phone

Email

Name

Address

City   State   Zip

Phone

Email

Name

Address

City   State   Zip

Phone

Email

Name

Address

City   State   Zip

Phone

Email

Contacts

Name

Address

City   State   Zip

Phone

Email

Name

Address

City   State   Zip

Phone

Email

Name

Address

City   State   Zip

Phone

Email

Name

Address

City   State   Zip

Phone

Email

Name

Address

City   State   Zip

Phone

Email

Name

Address

City   State   Zip

Phone

Email

Name

Address

City   State   Zip

Phone

Email

Name

Address

City   State   Zip

Phone

Email

Name

Address

City   State   Zip

Phone

Email

Name

Address

City   State   Zip

Phone

Email

Contacts

Name

Address

City   State   Zip

Phone

Email

Name

Address

City   State   Zip

Phone

Email

Name

Address

City   State   Zip

Phone

Email

Name

Address

City   State   Zip

Phone

Email

Name

Address

City   State   Zip

Phone

Email

Name

Address

City   State   Zip

Phone

Email

Name

Address

City   State   Zip

Phone

Email

Name

Address

City   State   Zip

Phone

Email

Name

Address

City   State   Zip

Phone

Email

Name

Address

City   State   Zip

Phone

Email

Contacts

Name

Address

City   State   Zip

Phone

Email

Name

Address

City   State   Zip

Phone

Email

Name

Address

City   State   Zip

Phone

Email

Name

Address

City   State   Zip

Phone

Email

Name

Address

City   State   Zip

Phone

Email

Name

Address

City   State   Zip

Phone

Email

Name

Address

City   State   Zip

Phone

Email

Name

Address

City   State   Zip

Phone

Email

Name

Address

City   State   Zip

Phone

Email

Name

Address

City   State   Zip

Phone

Email

Contacts

Name

Address

City   State   Zip

Phone

Email

Name

Address

City   State   Zip

Phone

Email

Name

Address

City   State   Zip

Phone

Email

Name

Address

City   State   Zip

Phone

Email

Name

Address

City   State   Zip

Phone

Email

Name

Address

City   State   Zip

Phone

Email

Name

Address

City   State   Zip

Phone

Email

Name

Address

City   State   Zip

Phone

Email

Name

Address

City   State   Zip

Phone

Email

Name

Address

City   State   Zip

Phone

Email

Contacts

Name

Address

City   State   Zip

Phone

Email

Name

Address

City   State   Zip

Phone

Email

Name

Address

City   State   Zip

Phone

Email

Name

Address

City   State   Zip

Phone

Email

Name

Address

City   State   Zip

Phone

Email

Name

Address

City   State   Zip

Phone

Email

Name

Address

City   State   Zip

Phone

Email

Name

Address

City   State   Zip

Phone

Email

Name

Address

City   State   Zip

Phone

Email

Name

Address

City   State   Zip

Phone

Email

Contacts

Name	**Name**
Address	Address
City State Zip	City State Zip
Phone	Phone
Email	Email
Name	**Name**
Address	Address
City State Zip	City State Zip
Phone	Phone
Email	Email
Name	**Name**
Address	Address
City State Zip	City State Zip
Phone	Phone
Email	Email
Name	**Name**
Address	Address
City State Zip	City State Zip
Phone	Phone
Email	Email
Name	**Name**
Address	Address
City State Zip	City State Zip
Phone	Phone
Email	Email

Contacts

Name

Address

City   State   Zip

Phone

Email

Name

Address

City   State   Zip

Phone

Email

Name

Address

City   State   Zip

Phone

Email

Name

Address

City   State   Zip

Phone

Email

Name

Address

City   State   Zip

Phone

Email

Name

Address

City   State   Zip

Phone

Email

Name

Address

City   State   Zip

Phone

Email

Name

Address

City   State   Zip

Phone

Email

Name

Address

City   State   Zip

Phone

Email

Name

Address

City   State   Zip

Phone

Email

Contacts

Name

Address

City   State   Zip

Phone

Email

Name

Address

City   State   Zip

Phone

Email

Name

Address

City   State   Zip

Phone

Email

Name

Address

City   State   Zip

Phone

Email

Name

Address

City   State   Zip

Phone

Email

Name

Address

City   State   Zip

Phone

Email

Name

Address

City   State   Zip

Phone

Email

Name

Address

City   State   Zip

Phone

Email

Name

Address

City   State   Zip

Phone

Email

Name

Address

City   State   Zip

Phone

Email

Contacts

Name

Address

City　　　　　State　　　Zip

Phone

Email

Name

Address

City　　　　　State　　　Zip

Phone

Email

Name

Address

City　　　　　State　　　Zip

Phone

Email

Name

Address

City　　　　　State　　　Zip

Phone

Email

Name

Address

City　　　　　State　　　Zip

Phone

Email

Name

Address

City　　　　　State　　　Zip

Phone

Email

Name

Address

City　　　　　State　　　Zip

Phone

Email

Name

Address

City　　　　　State　　　Zip

Phone

Email

Name

Address

City　　　　　State　　　Zip

Phone

Email

Name

Address

City　　　　　State　　　Zip

Phone

Email

Contacts

Name

Address

City   State   Zip

Phone

Email

Name

Address

City   State   Zip

Phone

Email

Name

Address

City   State   Zip

Phone

Email

Name

Address

City   State   Zip

Phone

Email

Name

Address

City   State   Zip

Phone

Email

Name

Address

City   State   Zip

Phone

Email

Name

Address

City   State   Zip

Phone

Email

Name

Address

City   State   Zip

Phone

Email

Name

Address

City   State   Zip

Phone

Email

Name

Address

City   State   Zip

Phone

Email

Contacts

Name

Address

City   State   Zip

Phone

Email

Name

Address

City   State   Zip

Phone

Email

Name

Address

City   State   Zip

Phone

Email

Name

Address

City   State   Zip

Phone

Email

Name

Address

City   State   Zip

Phone

Email

Name

Address

City   State   Zip

Phone

Email

Name

Address

City   State   Zip

Phone

Email

Name

Address

City   State   Zip

Phone

Email

Name

Address

City   State   Zip

Phone

Email

Name

Address

City   State   Zip

Phone

Email

Contacts

Name

Address

City   State   Zip

Phone

Email

Name

Address

City   State   Zip

Phone

Email

Name

Address

City   State   Zip

Phone

Email

Name

Address

City   State   Zip

Phone

Email

Name

Address

City   State   Zip

Phone

Email

Name

Address

City   State   Zip

Phone

Email

Name

Address

City   State   Zip

Phone

Email

Name

Address

City   State   Zip

Phone

Email

Name

Address

City   State   Zip

Phone

Email

Name

Address

City   State   Zip

Phone

Email

Contacts

Name

Address

City   State   Zip

Phone

Email

Name

Address

City   State   Zip

Phone

Email

Name

Address

City   State   Zip

Phone

Email

Name

Address

City   State   Zip

Phone

Email

Name

Address

City   State   Zip

Phone

Email

Name

Address

City   State   Zip

Phone

Email

Name

Address

City   State   Zip

Phone

Email

Name

Address

City   State   Zip

Phone

Email

Name

Address

City   State   Zip

Phone

Email

Name

Address

City   State   Zip

Phone

Email

Contacts

Name

Address

City .... State .... Zip

Phone

Email

Name

Address

City .... State .... Zip

Phone

Email

Name

Address

City .... State .... Zip

Phone

Email

Name

Address

City .... State .... Zip

Phone

Email

Name

Address

City .... State .... Zip

Phone

Email

Name

Address

City .... State .... Zip

Phone

Email

Name

Address

City .... State .... Zip

Phone

Email

Name

Address

City .... State .... Zip

Phone

Email

Name

Address

City .... State .... Zip

Phone

Email

Name

Address

City .... State .... Zip

Phone

Email

Contacts

Name

Address

City   State   Zip

Phone

Email

Name

Address

City   State   Zip

Phone

Email

Name

Address

City   State   Zip

Phone

Email

Name

Address

City   State   Zip

Phone

Email

Name

Address

City   State   Zip

Phone

Email

Name

Address

City   State   Zip

Phone

Email

Name

Address

City   State   Zip

Phone

Email

Name

Address

City   State   Zip

Phone

Email

Name

Address

City   State   Zip

Phone

Email

Name

Address

City   State   Zip

Phone

Email

Contacts

Name		
Address		
City	State	Zip
Phone		
Email		

Name		
Address		
City	State	Zip
Phone		
Email		

Name		
Address		
City	State	Zip
Phone		
Email		

Name		
Address		
City	State	Zip
Phone		
Email		

Name		
Address		
City	State	Zip
Phone		
Email		

Name		
Address		
City	State	Zip
Phone		
Email		

Name		
Address		
City	State	Zip
Phone		
Email		

Name		
Address		
City	State	Zip
Phone		
Email		

Name		
Address		
City	State	Zip
Phone		
Email		

Name		
Address		
City	State	Zip
Phone		
Email		

Contacts

Name

Address

City   State   Zip

Phone

Email

Name

Address

City   State   Zip

Phone

Email

Name

Address

City   State   Zip

Phone

Email

Name

Address

City   State   Zip

Phone

Email

Name

Address

City   State   Zip

Phone

Email

Name

Address

City   State   Zip

Phone

Email

Name

Address

City   State   Zip

Phone

Email

Name

Address

City   State   Zip

Phone

Email

Name

Address

City   State   Zip

Phone

Email

Name

Address

City   State   Zip

Phone

Email

Contacts

Name

Address

City   State   Zip

Phone

Email

Name

Address

City   State   Zip

Phone

Email

Name

Address

City   State   Zip

Phone

Email

Name

Address

City   State   Zip

Phone

Email

Name

Address

City   State   Zip

Phone

Email

Name

Address

City   State   Zip

Phone

Email

Name

Address

City   State   Zip

Phone

Email

Name

Address

City   State   Zip

Phone

Email

Name

Address

City   State   Zip

Phone

Email

Name

Address

City   State   Zip

Phone

Email

Contacts

Name

Address

City   State   Zip

Phone

Email

Name

Address

City   State   Zip

Phone

Email

Name

Address

City   State   Zip

Phone

Email

Name

Address

City   State   Zip

Phone

Email

Name

Address

City   State   Zip

Phone

Email

Name

Address

City   State   Zip

Phone

Email

Name

Address

City   State   Zip

Phone

Email

Name

Address

City   State   Zip

Phone

Email

Name

Address

City   State   Zip

Phone

Email

Name

Address

City   State   Zip

Phone

Email

Contacts

Name

Address

City   State   Zip

Phone

Email

Name

Address

City   State   Zip

Phone

Email

Name

Address

City   State   Zip

Phone

Email

Name

Address

City   State   Zip

Phone

Email

Name

Address

City   State   Zip

Phone

Email

Name

Address

City   State   Zip

Phone

Email

Name

Address

City   State   Zip

Phone

Email

Name

Address

City   State   Zip

Phone

Email

Name

Address

City   State   Zip

Phone

Email

Name

Address

City   State   Zip

Phone

Email

Contacts

Name

Address

City   State   Zip

Phone

Email

Name

Address

City   State   Zip

Phone

Email

Name

Address

City   State   Zip

Phone

Email

Name

Address

City   State   Zip

Phone

Email

Name

Address

City   State   Zip

Phone

Email

Name

Address

City   State   Zip

Phone

Email

Name

Address

City   State   Zip

Phone

Email

Name

Address

City   State   Zip

Phone

Email

Name

Address

City   State   Zip

Phone

Email

Name

Address

City   State   Zip

Phone

Email

Contacts

Name

Address

City   State   Zip

Phone

Email

Name

Address

City   State   Zip

Phone

Email

Name

Address

City   State   Zip

Phone

Email

Name

Address

City   State   Zip

Phone

Email

Name

Address

City   State   Zip

Phone

Email

Name

Address

City   State   Zip

Phone

Email

Name

Address

City   State   Zip

Phone

Email

Name

Address

City   State   Zip

Phone

Email

Name

Address

City   State   Zip

Phone

Email

Name

Address

City   State   Zip

Phone

Email

Contacts

Name

Address

City   State   Zip

Phone

Email

Name

Address

City   State   Zip

Phone

Email

Name

Address

City   State   Zip

Phone

Email

Name

Address

City   State   Zip

Phone

Email

Name

Address

City   State   Zip

Phone

Email

Name

Address

City   State   Zip

Phone

Email

Name

Address

City   State   Zip

Phone

Email

Name

Address

City   State   Zip

Phone

Email

Name

Address

City   State   Zip

Phone

Email

Name

Address

City   State   Zip

Phone

Email

Contacts

Name

Address

City   State   Zip

Phone

Email

Name

Address

City   State   Zip

Phone

Email

Name

Address

City   State   Zip

Phone

Email

Name

Address

City   State   Zip

Phone

Email

Name

Address

City   State   Zip

Phone

Email

Name

Address

City   State   Zip

Phone

Email

Name

Address

City   State   Zip

Phone

Email

Name

Address

City   State   Zip

Phone

Email

Name

Address

City   State   Zip

Phone

Email

Name

Address

City   State   Zip

Phone

Email

Contacts

Name

Address

City   State   Zip

Phone

Email

Name

Address

City   State   Zip

Phone

Email

Name

Address

City   State   Zip

Phone

Email

Name

Address

City   State   Zip

Phone

Email

Name

Address

City   State   Zip

Phone

Email

Name

Address

City   State   Zip

Phone

Email

Name

Address

City   State   Zip

Phone

Email

Name

Address

City   State   Zip

Phone

Email

Name

Address

City   State   Zip

Phone

Email

Name

Address

City   State   Zip

Phone

Email

Contacts

Name

Address

City   State   Zip

Phone

Email

Name

Address

City   State   Zip

Phone

Email

Name

Address

City   State   Zip

Phone

Email

Name

Address

City   State   Zip

Phone

Email

Name

Address

City   State   Zip

Phone

Email

Name

Address

City   State   Zip

Phone

Email

Name

Address

City   State   Zip

Phone

Email

Name

Address

City   State   Zip

Phone

Email

Name

Address

City   State   Zip

Phone

Email

Name

Address

City   State   Zip

Phone

Email

Contacts

Name

Address

City   State   Zip

Phone

Email

Name

Address

City   State   Zip

Phone

Email

Name

Address

City   State   Zip

Phone

Email

Name

Address

City   State   Zip

Phone

Email

Name

Address

City   State   Zip

Phone

Email

Name

Address

City   State   Zip

Phone

Email

Name

Address

City   State   Zip

Phone

Email

Name

Address

City   State   Zip

Phone

Email

Name

Address

City   State   Zip

Phone

Email

Name

Address

City   State   Zip

Phone

Email

Contacts

Name

Address

City   State   Zip

Phone

Email

Name

Address

City   State   Zip

Phone

Email

Name

Address

City   State   Zip

Phone

Email

Name

Address

City   State   Zip

Phone

Email

Name

Address

City   State   Zip

Phone

Email

Name

Address

City   State   Zip

Phone

Email

Name

Address

City   State   Zip

Phone

Email

Name

Address

City   State   Zip

Phone

Email

Name

Address

City   State   Zip

Phone

Email

Name

Address

City   State   Zip

Phone

Email

Contacts

Name

Address

City   State   Zip

Phone

Email

Name

Address

City   State   Zip

Phone

Email

Name

Address

City   State   Zip

Phone

Email

Name

Address

City   State   Zip

Phone

Email

Name

Address

City   State   Zip

Phone

Email

Name

Address

City   State   Zip

Phone

Email

Name

Address

City   State   Zip

Phone

Email

Name

Address

City   State   Zip

Phone

Email

Name

Address

City   State   Zip

Phone

Email

Name

Address

City   State   Zip

Phone

Email

Contacts

Name

Address

City   State   Zip

Phone

Email

Name

Address

City   State   Zip

Phone

Email

Name

Address

City   State   Zip

Phone

Email

Name

Address

City   State   Zip

Phone

Email

Name

Address

City   State   Zip

Phone

Email

Name

Address

City   State   Zip

Phone

Email

Name

Address

City   State   Zip

Phone

Email

Name

Address

City   State   Zip

Phone

Email

Name

Address

City   State   Zip

Phone

Email

Name

Address

City   State   Zip

Phone

Email

Contacts

Name

Address

City   State   Zip

Phone

Email

Name

Address

City   State   Zip

Phone

Email

Name

Address

City   State   Zip

Phone

Email

Name

Address

City   State   Zip

Phone

Email

Name

Address

City   State   Zip

Phone

Email

Name

Address

City   State   Zip

Phone

Email

Name

Address

City   State   Zip

Phone

Email

Name

Address

City   State   Zip

Phone

Email

Name

Address

City   State   Zip

Phone

Email

Name

Address

City   State   Zip

Phone

Email

Contacts

Name

Address

City   State   Zip

Phone

Email

Name

Address

City   State   Zip

Phone

Email

Name

Address

City   State   Zip

Phone

Email

Name

Address

City   State   Zip

Phone

Email

Name

Address

City   State   Zip

Phone

Email

Name

Address

City   State   Zip

Phone

Email

Name

Address

City   State   Zip

Phone

Email

Name

Address

City   State   Zip

Phone

Email

Name

Address

City   State   Zip

Phone

Email

Name

Address

City   State   Zip

Phone

Email

Contacts

Name

Address

City   State   Zip

Phone

Email

Name

Address

City   State   Zip

Phone

Email

Name

Address

City   State   Zip

Phone

Email

Name

Address

City   State   Zip

Phone

Email

Name

Address

City   State   Zip

Phone

Email

Name

Address

City   State   Zip

Phone

Email

Name

Address

City   State   Zip

Phone

Email

Name

Address

City   State   Zip

Phone

Email

Name

Address

City   State   Zip

Phone

Email

Name

Address

City   State   Zip

Phone

Email

Contacts

Name

Address

City   State   Zip

Phone

Email

Name

Address

City   State   Zip

Phone

Email

Name

Address

City   State   Zip

Phone

Email

Name

Address

City   State   Zip

Phone

Email

Name

Address

City   State   Zip

Phone

Email

Name

Address

City   State   Zip

Phone

Email

Name

Address

City   State   Zip

Phone

Email

Name

Address

City   State   Zip

Phone

Email

Name

Address

City   State   Zip

Phone

Email

Name

Address

City   State   Zip

Phone

Email

Contacts

Name

Address

City   State   Zip

Phone

Email

Name

Address

City   State   Zip

Phone

Email

Name

Address

City   State   Zip

Phone

Email

Name

Address

City   State   Zip

Phone

Email

Name

Address

City   State   Zip

Phone

Email

Name

Address

City   State   Zip

Phone

Email

Name

Address

City   State   Zip

Phone

Email

Name

Address

City   State   Zip

Phone

Email

Name

Address

City   State   Zip

Phone

Email

Name

Address

City   State   Zip

Phone

Email

Contacts

Name

Address

City   State   Zip

Phone

Email

Name

Address

City   State   Zip

Phone

Email

Name

Address

City   State   Zip

Phone

Email

Name

Address

City   State   Zip

Phone

Email

Name

Address

City   State   Zip

Phone

Email

Name

Address

City   State   Zip

Phone

Email

Name

Address

City   State   Zip

Phone

Email

Name

Address

City   State   Zip

Phone

Email

Name

Address

City   State   Zip

Phone

Email

Name

Address

City   State   Zip

Phone

Email

Contacts

Name

Address

City   State   Zip

Phone

Email

Name

Address

City   State   Zip

Phone

Email

Name

Address

City   State   Zip

Phone

Email

Name

Address

City   State   Zip

Phone

Email

Name

Address

City   State   Zip

Phone

Email

Name

Address

City   State   Zip

Phone

Email

Name

Address

City   State   Zip

Phone

Email

Name

Address

City   State   Zip

Phone

Email

Name

Address

City   State   Zip

Phone

Email

Name

Address

City   State   Zip

Phone

Email

Contacts

Name

Address

City   State   Zip

Phone

Email

Name

Address

City   State   Zip

Phone

Email

Name

Address

City   State   Zip

Phone

Email

Name

Address

City   State   Zip

Phone

Email

Name

Address

City   State   Zip

Phone

Email

Name

Address

City   State   Zip

Phone

Email

Name

Address

City   State   Zip

Phone

Email

Name

Address

City   State   Zip

Phone

Email

Name

Address

City   State   Zip

Phone

Email

Name

Address

City   State   Zip

Phone

Email

Contacts

Name

Address

City   State   Zip

Phone

Email

Name

Address

City   State   Zip

Phone

Email

Name

Address

City   State   Zip

Phone

Email

Name

Address

City   State   Zip

Phone

Email

Name

Address

City   State   Zip

Phone

Email

Name

Address

City   State   Zip

Phone

Email

Name

Address

City   State   Zip

Phone

Email

Name

Address

City   State   Zip

Phone

Email

Name

Address

City   State   Zip

Phone

Email

Name

Address

City   State   Zip

Phone

Email

Contacts

Name

Address

City   State   Zip

Phone

Email

Name

Address

City   State   Zip

Phone

Email

Name

Address

City   State   Zip

Phone

Email

Name

Address

City   State   Zip

Phone

Email

Name

Address

City   State   Zip

Phone

Email

Name

Address

City   State   Zip

Phone

Email

Name

Address

City   State   Zip

Phone

Email

Name

Address

City   State   Zip

Phone

Email

Name

Address

City   State   Zip

Phone

Email

Name

Address

City   State   Zip

Phone

Email

Contacts

Name

Address

City   State   Zip

Phone

Email

Name

Address

City   State   Zip

Phone

Email

Name

Address

City   State   Zip

Phone

Email

Name

Address

City   State   Zip

Phone

Email

Name

Address

City   State   Zip

Phone

Email

Name

Address

City   State   Zip

Phone

Email

Name

Address

City   State   Zip

Phone

Email

Name

Address

City   State   Zip

Phone

Email

Name

Address

City   State   Zip

Phone

Email

Name

Address

City   State   Zip

Phone

Email

Contacts

Name

Address

City   State   Zip

Phone

Email

Name

Address

City   State   Zip

Phone

Email

Name

Address

City   State   Zip

Phone

Email

Name

Address

City   State   Zip

Phone

Email

Name

Address

City   State   Zip

Phone

Email

Name

Address

City   State   Zip

Phone

Email

Name

Address

City   State   Zip

Phone

Email

Name

Address

City   State   Zip

Phone

Email

Name

Address

City   State   Zip

Phone

Email

Name

Address

City   State   Zip

Phone

Email

Contacts

Name

Address

City   State   Zip

Phone

Email

Name

Address

City   State   Zip

Phone

Email

Name

Address

City   State   Zip

Phone

Email

Name

Address

City   State   Zip

Phone

Email

Name

Address

City   State   Zip

Phone

Email

Name

Address

City   State   Zip

Phone

Email

Name

Address

City   State   Zip

Phone

Email

Name

Address

City   State   Zip

Phone

Email

Name

Address

City   State   Zip

Phone

Email

Name

Address

City   State   Zip

Phone

Email

Contacts

Name

Address

City　　　　　State　　　Zip

Phone

Email

Name

Address

City　　　　　State　　　Zip

Phone

Email

Name

Address

City　　　　　State　　　Zip

Phone

Email

Name

Address

City　　　　　State　　　Zip

Phone

Email

Name

Address

City　　　　　State　　　Zip

Phone

Email

Name

Address

City　　　　　State　　　Zip

Phone

Email

Name

Address

City　　　　　State　　　Zip

Phone

Email

Name

Address

City　　　　　State　　　Zip

Phone

Email

Name

Address

City　　　　　State　　　Zip

Phone

Email

Name

Address

City　　　　　State　　　Zip

Phone

Email

Contacts

Name	**Name**
Address	Address
City State Zip	City State Zip
Phone	Phone
Email	Email
Name	**Name**
Address	Address
City State Zip	City State Zip
Phone	Phone
Email	Email
Name	**Name**
Address	Address
City State Zip	City State Zip
Phone	Phone
Email	Email
Name	**Name**
Address	Address
City State Zip	City State Zip
Phone	Phone
Email	Email
Name	**Name**
Address	Address
City State Zip	City State Zip
Phone	Phone
Email	Email

Contacts

Name

Address

City　　　　　　State　　　Zip

Phone

Email

Name

Address

City　　　　　　State　　　Zip

Phone

Email

Name

Address

City　　　　　　State　　　Zip

Phone

Email

Name

Address

City　　　　　　State　　　Zip

Phone

Email

Name

Address

City　　　　　　State　　　Zip

Phone

Email

Name

Address

City　　　　　　State　　　Zip

Phone

Email

Name

Address

City　　　　　　State　　　Zip

Phone

Email

Name

Address

City　　　　　　State　　　Zip

Phone

Email

Name

Address

City　　　　　　State　　　Zip

Phone

Email

Name

Address

City　　　　　　State　　　Zip

Phone

Email

Contacts

Name			Name		
Address			Address		
City	State	Zip	City	State	Zip
Phone			Phone		
Email			Email		

Name			Name		
Address			Address		
City	State	Zip	City	State	Zip
Phone			Phone		
Email			Email		

Name			Name		
Address			Address		
City	State	Zip	City	State	Zip
Phone			Phone		
Email			Email		

Name			Name		
Address			Address		
City	State	Zip	City	State	Zip
Phone			Phone		
Email			Email		

Name			Name		
Address			Address		
City	State	Zip	City	State	Zip
Phone			Phone		
Email			Email		

Contacts

Name

Address

City   State   Zip

Phone

Email

Name

Address

City   State   Zip

Phone

Email

Name

Address

City   State   Zip

Phone

Email

Name

Address

City   State   Zip

Phone

Email

Name

Address

City   State   Zip

Phone

Email

Name

Address

City   State   Zip

Phone

Email

Name

Address

City   State   Zip

Phone

Email

Name

Address

City   State   Zip

Phone

Email

Name

Address

City   State   Zip

Phone

Email

Name

Address

City   State   Zip

Phone

Email

Contacts

Name	**Name**
Address	Address
City State Zip	City State Zip
Phone	Phone
Email	Email
Name	**Name**
Address	Address
City State Zip	City State Zip
Phone	Phone
Email	Email
Name	**Name**
Address	Address
City State Zip	City State Zip
Phone	Phone
Email	Email
Name	**Name**
Address	Address
City State Zip	City State Zip
Phone	Phone
Email	Email
Name	**Name**
Address	Address
City State Zip	City State Zip
Phone	Phone
Email	Email

Contacts

Name

Address

City   State   Zip

Phone

Email

Name

Address

City   State   Zip

Phone

Email

Name

Address

City   State   Zip

Phone

Email

Name

Address

City   State   Zip

Phone

Email

Name

Address

City   State   Zip

Phone

Email

Name

Address

City   State   Zip

Phone

Email

Name

Address

City   State   Zip

Phone

Email

Name

Address

City   State   Zip

Phone

Email

Name

Address

City   State   Zip

Phone

Email

Name

Address

City   State   Zip

Phone

Email

Contacts

Name			Name		
Address			Address		
City	State	Zip	City	State	Zip
Phone			Phone		
Email			Email		

Name			Name		
Address			Address		
City	State	Zip	City	State	Zip
Phone			Phone		
Email			Email		

Name			Name		
Address			Address		
City	State	Zip	City	State	Zip
Phone			Phone		
Email			Email		

Name			Name		
Address			Address		
City	State	Zip	City	State	Zip
Phone			Phone		
Email			Email		

Name			Name		
Address			Address		
City	State	Zip	City	State	Zip
Phone			Phone		
Email			Email		

Contacts

Name

Address

City   State   Zip

Phone

Email

Name

Address

City   State   Zip

Phone

Email

Name

Address

City   State   Zip

Phone

Email

Name

Address

City   State   Zip

Phone

Email

Name

Address

City   State   Zip

Phone

Email

Name

Address

City   State   Zip

Phone

Email

Name

Address

City   State   Zip

Phone

Email

Name

Address

City   State   Zip

Phone

Email

Name

Address

City   State   Zip

Phone

Email

Name

Address

City   State   Zip

Phone

Email

Contacts

Name

Address

City   State   Zip

Phone

Email

Name

Address

City   State   Zip

Phone

Email

Name

Address

City   State   Zip

Phone

Email

Name

Address

City   State   Zip

Phone

Email

Name

Address

City   State   Zip

Phone

Email

Name

Address

City   State   Zip

Phone

Email

Name

Address

City   State   Zip

Phone

Email

Name

Address

City   State   Zip

Phone

Email

Name

Address

City   State   Zip

Phone

Email

Name

Address

City   State   Zip

Phone

Email

Contacts

Name

Address

City   State   Zip

Phone

Email

Name

Address

City   State   Zip

Phone

Email

Name

Address

City   State   Zip

Phone

Email

Name

Address

City   State   Zip

Phone

Email

Name

Address

City   State   Zip

Phone

Email

Name

Address

City   State   Zip

Phone

Email

Name

Address

City   State   Zip

Phone

Email

Name

Address

City   State   Zip

Phone

Email

Name

Address

City   State   Zip

Phone

Email

Name

Address

City   State   Zip

Phone

Email

Contacts

Name	**Name**
Address	Address
City State Zip	City State Zip
Phone	Phone
Email	Email
Name	**Name**
Address	Address
City State Zip	City State Zip
Phone	Phone
Email	Email
Name	**Name**
Address	Address
City State Zip	City State Zip
Phone	Phone
Email	Email
Name	**Name**
Address	Address
City State Zip	City State Zip
Phone	Phone
Email	Email
Name	**Name**
Address	Address
City State Zip	City State Zip
Phone	Phone
Email	Email

Contacts

Name

Address

City   State   Zip

Phone

Email

Name

Address

City   State   Zip

Phone

Email

Name

Address

City   State   Zip

Phone

Email

Name

Address

City   State   Zip

Phone

Email

Name

Address

City   State   Zip

Phone

Email

Name

Address

City   State   Zip

Phone

Email

Name

Address

City   State   Zip

Phone

Email

Name

Address

City   State   Zip

Phone

Email

Name

Address

City   State   Zip

Phone

Email

Name

Address

City   State   Zip

Phone

Email

Contacts

Name	**Name**
Address	Address
City State Zip	City State Zip
Phone	Phone
Email	Email
Name	**Name**
Address	Address
City State Zip	City State Zip
Phone	Phone
Email	Email
Name	**Name**
Address	Address
City State Zip	City State Zip
Phone	Phone
Email	Email
Name	**Name**
Address	Address
City State Zip	City State Zip
Phone	Phone
Email	Email
Name	**Name**
Address	Address
City State Zip	City State Zip
Phone	Phone
Email	Email

Contacts

Name

Address

City   State   Zip

Phone

Email

Name

Address

City   State   Zip

Phone

Email

Name

Address

City   State   Zip

Phone

Email

Name

Address

City   State   Zip

Phone

Email

Name

Address

City   State   Zip

Phone

Email

Name

Address

City   State   Zip

Phone

Email

Name

Address

City   State   Zip

Phone

Email

Name

Address

City   State   Zip

Phone

Email

Name

Address

City   State   Zip

Phone

Email

Name

Address

City   State   Zip

Phone

Email

Contacts

Name

Address

City   State   Zip

Phone

Email

Name

Address

City   State   Zip

Phone

Email

Name

Address

City   State   Zip

Phone

Email

Name

Address

City   State   Zip

Phone

Email

Name

Address

City   State   Zip

Phone

Email

Name

Address

City   State   Zip

Phone

Email

Name

Address

City   State   Zip

Phone

Email

Name

Address

City   State   Zip

Phone

Email

Name

Address

City   State   Zip

Phone

Email

Name

Address

City   State   Zip

Phone

Email

Contacts

Name

Address

City   State   Zip

Phone

Email

Name

Address

City   State   Zip

Phone

Email

Name

Address

City   State   Zip

Phone

Email

Name

Address

City   State   Zip

Phone

Email

Name

Address

City   State   Zip

Phone

Email

Name

Address

City   State   Zip

Phone

Email

Name

Address

City   State   Zip

Phone

Email

Name

Address

City   State   Zip

Phone

Email

Name

Address

City   State   Zip

Phone

Email

Name

Address

City   State   Zip

Phone

Email

Contacts

Name

Address

City   State   Zip

Phone

Email

Name

Address

City   State   Zip

Phone

Email

Name

Address

City   State   Zip

Phone

Email

Name

Address

City   State   Zip

Phone

Email

Name

Address

City   State   Zip

Phone

Email

Name

Address

City   State   Zip

Phone

Email

Name

Address

City   State   Zip

Phone

Email

Name

Address

City   State   Zip

Phone

Email

Name

Address

City   State   Zip

Phone

Email

Name

Address

City   State   Zip

Phone

Email

Contacts

Name

Address

City   State   Zip

Phone

Email

Name

Address

City   State   Zip

Phone

Email

Name

Address

City   State   Zip

Phone

Email

Name

Address

City   State   Zip

Phone

Email

Name

Address

City   State   Zip

Phone

Email

Name

Address

City   State   Zip

Phone

Email

Name

Address

City   State   Zip

Phone

Email

Name

Address

City   State   Zip

Phone

Email

Name

Address

City   State   Zip

Phone

Email

Name

Address

City   State   Zip

Phone

Email

Made in the USA
Monee, IL
27 June 2022

98722362R00063